ISTP:

Understand And Break Free From Your Own Limitations

MATTHEW BRIGHTHOUSE

Copyright © 2017

Table of Contents

1
Introduction

By taking the Briggs Myers Personality Test, you are able to identify your particular personality type. Of course, you already know this, because the chances are you have already done that and you came up with the ISTP personality type as your result!

You are the Virtuoso, you are someone who loves to explore, you are creative, you don't mind getting your hands dirty, and you adore finding out how things work. Put simply, you're a pretty handy person to have around! You are also quite rare, as you only make up around 5% of the general population, so you're certainly one of a kind!

The main point of taking the Briggs Myers Personality Test is to be able to identify your personality type and then learn from it, finding out your strengths and weaknesses, and taking on board information which helps you develop into a seriously awesome, rounded person! It's important to realize that by learning more about your personality type, you are never going to become a 'perfect' person because quite frankly that type of person simply doesn't exist. What the information you learn does allow you to do however is highlight your strengths, so you can learn to use them for even more good, and also to identify your weaknesses, so you can work on them and learn. Over time, this will help you strike out and really reach your overall potential, without limitations holding you back.

The other important thing to note is that nobody is ever 100% one particular personality type. If you found yourself having to really think about your choices when taking the test, perhaps torn between a couple of options, then the chances are you have tendencies of another personality type too. It is a good idea to learn about all the personality types to some degree, because you may find hints of yourself in another type, and you can use that information to further develop yourself. The other useful point in learning about the personality types overall is that it helps you to understand other people much better too. If you are working in a management type of role, this is very useful indeed. People management really depends on how you understand your staff, but even if you are not in that type of role, your social relationships and how you interact with other people will be greatly improved by knowing why certain people act and react the way they do.

If you take anything away from this book, let it be that there is no criticism intended. When we are embarking on a self-discovery journey, it's vital to be totally honest. When we are talking about your ISTP personality type, we are going to highlight your strengths, big you up a little and let you puff your chest out in pride, but we're also going to tell you the things that aren't so great about your personality type. You might have this point in your personality to a large degree, or it could just be a hint, but either way, it's important to take it as constructive, and not personal.

We are here to help, not drag you down!

Throughout this book, you will see that the ISTP personality type has many upsides, and it has a few downsides too, but even the downsides can be twisted around to become positives! This is the same with every personality type on the spectrum. Human beings are flawed from the start, but those flaws are what make us interesting and different. If we were all the same, can you imagine how boring life would be? Yawn-Ville! By having these weaknesses, we become interesting and challenging. But the key is to know about them, so you can stop them from being massive negatives, which may have a poor impact on your life, and your relationships with other people.

Now you know the aim of this book, and you know exactly what we're trying to achieve, it's time to put the process into action. So, if you're ready to learn more about your creative and interesting ISTP personality type, then turn the page and get ready to be enlightened!

2
The Fine Line Between Strength and Weakness

We all have strengths and we all have weaknesses; this is what makes us human beings. If we were simply full of strengths, and we didn't have the slightest weakness to own up to, life would be very boring indeed! We learn important life lessons from our weaknesses, so it is important to know what they are, so they can be improved upon to some degree.

The whole point of any self-discovery journey is to understand the full story, good, bad, and everything in-between.

We know that you are an ISTP personality type, but first things first, what does that stand for?

I = Introvert
S = Sensing
T = Thinking
P = Perception

Let's break that down a little, to explain in more detail.

Introversion

You are not an extrovert, you are not someone who is always in the center of the crowd, loud and proud, you are someone who is quiet, standing on the fringes. This makes you an introvert. In terms of the personality types, introversion describes someone who is more about logic and thinking, than someone who is vocal and outgoing. That doesn't mean that you are not confident, instead, it means that you are quietly so and that in many ways is a strength in itself.

The downside of being an introvert, however, is that you can sometimes dip down too far into your shell, and people can find it difficult to get you to open up, so they can really get to know you. This is something we are going to talk about in more detail as our book goes on, to allow you to learn how to let other people into your inner sanctuary, without upsetting your own quiet balance.

Sensing

Sensing goes hand in hand with introversion. You are not someone who is loud, as we mentioned, and instead, you are much more likely to feel something. Despite that, you are quite logical too. You are somewhat of a contradiction and enigma in many ways, but your curiosity and eagerness to work out how things tick is something which leads you down some interesting routes in life. The problem you do sometimes encounter is allowing yourself to become emotionally stuck, e.g. you don't find it easy to let others know how you feel. This is something you can work on, and also something we are going to cover in a later 'how to' chapter – never fear!

Another important part of what makes up the ISTP personality type is the tendency to be calm one minute, and then hugely spontaneous the next. Whilst spontaneity is the spice of life, it is also important to try and rein it in a little at the same time. If you can do this, and if you can keep your cool in difficult situations, you will be able to channel that energy into more useful endeavors.

Thinking

We mentioned that you have a logical mind, and you like to know how things work. You are someone who will take something apart, just to learn more about it, not caring about getting your hands dirty. The downside is that you won't bother to put it back together again afterward, you will simply move onto the next thing! The ISTP mind is never still, it is always moving, always thinking, always trying to learn something new, and come up with a new endeavor to get stuck into. You are someone who soaks up knowledge like a sponge.

You love to create, you love to learn, and you love to come up with trial and error solutions to problems. A related area you can work on here is to learn to finish one task before you begin another. In a lot of ways, this is down to curbing your spontaneity, as we mentioned before, and this is something which is very do-able as part of your self-discovery journey.

Perception

The perception part of your personality type shows that you are not a judgmental type of individual, and instead, you are quite open and flexible. Whilst you have strong ideas and opinions, you are quite easy going in the fact that you accept that not everyone has to agree with you. This is a strength and something which you should be very proud of as part of your personality. The danger, however, is coming across to others as too laid back, and perhaps not caring. This isn't your intention, but it is vital to perhaps open up your emotions just a tad, to ensure that other people don't take your laid back, easy going nature, the wrong way.

Now we know what your personality type stands for, let's explore your strengths and weaknesses, to really understand your ISTP personality type a little more. Because we always try and be as positive as possible, let's start by bigging up your strengths!

ISTP Strengths

You are an optimistic soul

Because you don't take yourself too seriously, you tend to be quite positive in your outlook on life. This optimism is catching, and those people who you do let into your inner circle, find this to be one of your major plus points. When you are around people, they feel your energy and your optimism, and this lifts others up, rather than bringing them down.

In our weaknesses section, we will talk about the fact that you are quite a difficult person to get to know because you are so private. Your optimistic and fun nature is only revealed to those who you trust enough to show it to. If you can work on opening up a little more, you can share your joy and excitement with more people!

You have plentiful energy

Along with your optimism in general, you are also bounding in energy! Keeping up with you can be quite difficult for many people, and you are always on the go, trying to learn something, trying to find out how something works, and coming up with creative ways to spend your time. You're certainly not a bore to be around!

You do have a tendency to move from project to project, sometimes not finishing the first one before starting on another! This is a side effect of your boundless energy!

You are quite a rational person

You don't tend to be irrational very easily, and instead, you think about all sides of a situation before coming up with your course of action. Your spontaneous nature is something you need to curb occasionally, but this can be used as a strength too. You are able to keep it to one side until you need it the most, and you are usually able to surprise quite a few people with it too!

The fact that you are so laid back, something we will talk about later, this means you don't become ruffled or upset by the actions of others very easily. This is a plus point because it means less stress in your life overall, and that is always a good thing!

You are a great person to have around in a sticky situation

Your mixture of enthusiasm, spontaneity, rational thinking and eagerness to get your hands dirty and dig into a situation makes you the best person to have around in a difficult situation or even a crisis. You will work tirelessly to fix the situation because you hate to be defeated, and you won't hesitate to come up with creative answers either. Whilst other people will shy away from the rather challenging ways to solve a problem, the ways which involve rolling up their sleeve and really digging in deep, you don't hesitate to simply throw yourself into it. You pride yourself on solving the issue, and others are extremely grateful for this.

You are laid-back and chilled out

As we have already briefly mentioned, you're not someone who gets stressed out easily, and you prefer to let life happen, let the flow take you wherever it wants you to go. You don't worry too much about the future, and this is a positive thing because it doesn't cause you distress or worry; you just let it happen. Of course, you need to make plans occasionally, otherwise, life will not really take you anywhere meaningful, and this is something you need to keep an eye on, to ensure you're not so laid back you're practically horizontal!

ISTP Weaknesses

Now we have talked about what a wonderful human being you are, having celebrated your strengths, it's time to identify your weaknesses, so we can work on minimizing any negative effects they may have on your life overall. Remember that there is no judgment here, simply an acknowledgment of the fact that none of us are perfect, and that we can always work on our weaknesses, provided we are aware of them.

You have a tendency to be a little stubborn

Being a creative person, when you get the bit between your teeth, and you want to try and figure out how something working, you can be rather stubborn in your approach. You are so single-minded at times that you lose sight of everything else that is going on around you. Whilst this tenacity is an admirable trait in many ways, it's important to try and see all sides of a situation and perhaps compromise, just a little. If you can do this, you will be able to get to the bottom of the situation or project with ease, and you won't cause any other issues unwittingly along the way.

You also have a tendency to be a tad insensitive from time to time
You're not really that tuned into your own emotions, so you find it hard to really tune into anyone else's too. This can sometimes lead you to be insensitive. Of course, you don't mean to be; you are not a vindictive person, and you are not someone who likes to hurt others. This is something you can work on, to minimize any negative effects, and we will talk about this in a later chapter, to help you reach your goal. It's important to understand that emotions and feelings are part of being human, and if you can do this, and if you can learn to appreciate them for the wonderful things they are, you'll easily be able to curb this issue and stop it from being a problem in the future.

You can be very hard to get to know and understand

You don't let anyone in. It's not that you're untrusting, it's just that you're in your own little world, and you're quite private too. Those who you do let inside, are rewarded with someone who is creative, warm, and caring, but you need to drop your guard a little, to allow people to see that warmer side of you. You don't see the use in allowing just anyone to see who you are, you like to know that you can trust and understand someone before you allow them in. Again, we're going to talk about this in a later chapter, to help you open up a little, and let other people see you as the wonderful person you are. It certainly won't be easy to open up at first, because you're so used t your private and reserved ways, that it can be difficult to change. This isn't impossible, however, and again, it's about awareness. Once you know the issue, you can change it!

You're not big on commitment

Romantic relationships can be difficult for you as an ISTP because you are not a big fan of commitment. This really goes hand in hand with one of your strengths, because you are that laid back that plans just aren't your thing. You like to see where life takes you, you don't like to decide what you're going to do in the future. The problem with that is, if you meet someone who wants to make plans for the future, e.g. they want to know if your relationship is going to progress, your unwillingness to plan may be a reason for them to give up and walk away. Understanding that life sometimes has to be planned, and that

sometimes we do have to make commitments, is a
way of allowing that brick wall to fall. Commitment
isn't suffocating or upsetting, it is a way to share
yourself and your life with another person, and that in
itself is a wonderful thing.

**Your spontaneous nature can sometimes lead
you into trouble**

We have talked already about how you are
spontaneous, and whilst this is a great feature of your
personality, it can sometimes lead you into trouble.
Learning when it's okay to be spontaneous and when
it's best to not be is something you can work on. It's
not unusual for an ISTP personality to be
spontaneous and make a decision simply to see what
happens, without really thinking about the
consequences. There's a difference between taking
calculated risks, and flying by the seat of your pants!
Questioning your choices before going for it, can be
enough to help you understand whether this choice is
worth it, or one which is probably best passed over
for something safer.

As you can see, there are some fantastic strengths
there, and a few weaknesses to work on. Part of any
self-discovery journey is appreciating the balance. As
human beings we are part wonderful and part flawed;
this is what makes us who we are. Whilst it's
impossible to totally eradicate your weaknesses to
nothing, it is totally possible to work on them, so they
can be minimized in terms of the negative effect on
your life. It's also important to realize that you
shouldn't want to eradicate your weaknesses
completely anyway! If you're perfect, you're boring,

it's really that simple. It's about minimizing rather than ridding completely. Plus, does perfection really exist? I don't think so…

Throughout the rest of this book, we're going to talk about a few key areas you can work on, in order to help push your personality towards the best it can be. Nothing in this book is meant to be critical, and instead, it is meant to help you learn. We will keep reiterating that fact, simply because it's so important! Self-discovery isn't about pointing the finger and wagging them in scolding, it's about understanding and changing, tweaking details to create a more harmonious life for you, and for others around you too. If you can make these changes, you're knocking down walls, you're stopping weaknesses from limiting where you going in life, and doors will open!

So, without further ado, let's start with our first 'learn' chapter!

3
Learn to Tap Into Your Emotions

Despite your creative nature, you are not someone who uses your emotions to make decisions, and instead, you stick to logic. Whilst there is nothing wrong with this at all because logic is certainly there for a reason, it's important to understand that emotions are also there for a reason too.

Let's use mother's intuition as an example here. A mother listens to their inner voice, their gut feelings, to know when something is wrong, to know when to make a change, and to know what the right course of action is. It is a feeling, a 'yes this is right', and 'no this is wrong' feeling. Mother's intuition is one of the most powerful things on the planet.

Whilst you can't really say that intuition is a true emotion, it is a way of listening to your inner voice, tuning in to what your gut tells you, to help you make decisions and be warned of anything which just doesn't feel quite right. As an ISTP, you don't tend to be that open to your intuition generally. Another example is in terms of dealing with people. If you can turn that tuning knob, and get the frequency right, giving you the option to listen to that radio station when you need a little 'otherworldly' advice.

We mentioned in our weaknesses section that you can sometimes come across as insensitive because you simply don't realize that you're saying or doing something which may hurt someone else's feelings. Again, this isn't a finger pointing exercise, remember that right now!

As an ISTP, you are not a vindictive person, you are actually very warm once people get to know you but you use that logical mind of yours to think in all areas of your life. If you can just open up your mind and tap into your emotions a little, you can knock that potential insensitive streak on the head, and cut out any issues that may occur because of it.

For instance, if you unintentionally hurt someone you cared about, you would be mortified, but you probably wouldn't realize it at the time. What you say, you don't mean it to come across the way it does sometimes. However, someone who is more emotionally charged than you may take it another way entirely. This is where misunderstandings and problems can occur.

So, how can you learn to tap into those emotions of yours?

Bear Grylls, the popular TV personality, is an ISTP personality type. Bear is someone who uses his survival skills to get by, someone who uses his logic to survive in the roughest of circumstances. Do you think Bear uses his gut instinct? He has to in many ways, because sometimes just feeling that something is 'off' is the way to survive too. Despite his logical thinking, Bear has developed his emotions, to allow him to survive in the wilderness. Knowing how to understand your intuition, and to use it as a credible part of your 'go-to' armory is something you should certainly have at your disposal, just like Bear does.

You can do it too.

Basically, you need to try and think a different way. We don't want to turn off that logical thinking switch because it is there for a reason and has served you very well over the years. What we need to do, is try and give you an alternative switch, which you can use from time to time. It's a useful tool, we think you'll agree, and once you use it a few times, you'll see it for yourself in practice.

Think about a situation you have encountered this very day. It could be from work, it could be from generally going about your business, but is there any part of your day where you encountered another person? For instance, were you having a conversation at work about a project, and you had to give feedback to someone on their performance? Just as an example?

How did the person respond to your chat? Were they excited? Did they seem happy? Or, were they a little putout or quiet about what you had to say? Would you have been upset if someone said the same thing to you?

Once you have identified their response, try and think about why they may have felt that way. What did you say to them exactly? Now, turn it around, and think about how you would feel if those words were said to you, in the way they were said. It's likely that you wouldn't be bothered at all because as an ISTP, you simply don't think in the emotional way that others do, but it's important to realize that there are other personality types out there who are much more emotionally charged than you are.

These more emotionally charged people are not weak in any way, they are just built in a more emotional way than you are. Those people may see your logical side as a weakness, but it's certainly not. As you can see, it's about our own personal way of seeing things, and how we consider it to be important in our own lives, or otherwise.

Thinking back to that situation we were just picturing, what could you have done differently? Put yourself back in that situation and change the outcome by thinking about how you could have approached it in an alternative way.

By identifying these situations as they arise, and thinking them through with the help and benefit of hindsight, you can start to tweak your responses in the future. By doing this, you should be able to begin minimizing the frequency in which these instances happen.

Why Are Emotions So Important?

Human beings are designed to feel a huge range of different emotions, and this is what makes us who we are. There are those who are more emotionally sensitive than others, and those who are hiding their feelings quite well, preferring not to show to the outside world whatever it is they are experiencing on the inside. Whichever camp you fall into, and as an

ISTP, its likely that you simply don't register emotions on the same scale as others, emotions are vital to life.

Feeling an emotion does not make you weak, it makes you human. All emotions are a vital part of our existence. By nature, some of us are more attuned to them. This doesn't mean the rest of us are robotic, emotionless beings.

Rage, anger, upset, disappointment, fear, worry, anxiety, happiness, joy, humor, pride, jealousy, these are all emotions, and there are countless more besides. If we didn't feel these emotions, life would be a long haul of nothingness. Whilst negative emotions can be hurtful, positive emotions can be wonderful too.

I like to see emotions as our personal compass. If we regularly feel negative emotions, it's a clear indicator that something needs changing for us to get back on course. Furthermore, if we consistently feel positive emotions, we know that we are more in alignment with where we want to be.

Now, it's important to point out that as an ISTP you are certainly not devoid of all feeling, it's just that you don't always allow yourself to open up to the greatest degree, instead preferring to think in a logical and systematic way. It's also possible that you do feel these emotions, you just don't let anyone else know about it.

The thing is, if you can learn how to open up a little, by following the exercise we mentioned above, you

can not only learn how to deal with other people
much better, but you can bring a whole spectrum of
new feelings into your life too.

4

Learn to Open up And Allow People to Get to Know You

This next chapter really follows on perfectly from our first one, because learning how to be more emotional and learning how to open up generally, work together really well. If you can master the two, you're seriously on the way to self-discovery success.

As an ISTP, you are not an easy person to get to know. You are an enigma, you are a private and reserved person, but underneath it all, you're a wonderful and fun person too. If you can allow others to break through that outer shell on occasion, you will be able to enhance the relationships and friendships in your life beyond measure. You'll also feel much more positivity and joy as a result of allowing these relationships into your life, whether they stay there, or whether they serve their purpose and leave, to allow room for someone else to enter into your domain.

Some of this is down to trust, and some of it is simply down to being a private person. There is certainly nothing wrong with keeping your inner circle small because let's face it, the bigger your circle, the more stress there is likely to be! Having said that, if you don't let people get to know who you are, then you might be missing out on some seriously wonderful experiences, and a possible soul mate too!

Now, it's not in your nature to simply be open and honest with every single person who comes into your life, but if you can be choosy and perhaps just allow yourself to shine through a little more, you'll soon reap the benefits.

Perhaps the biggest problem for ISTPs, in this case, is the fact that if you are constantly closed off to meeting new people, then how do you know that you're not letting the love of your life slip by? Romantic relationships require us to be vulnerable and less private, which is something you find difficult generally. This is all a huge contradiction when you think about how you can also be massively spontaneous from time to time! You are never usually spontaneous when it comes to people, however, just situations.

Clint Eastwood is an ISTP personality type. Clint is not someone we really know that much about in terms of his personal life because he is so private. Perhaps that is a blessing in his line of work because it stops intrusion that would otherwise be unbearable. You are like Clint, but with less of the paparazzi (hopefully!).

So, how can you open up and let people get to know the real you, without feeling exposed?

It's not easy because you probably don't even realize you're doing it in many ways. You're often so focused on the task you're working on, i.e. trying to figure out how something works, that you don't really see what's going on around you. Take the time to see the people who are around you on a day to day basis. Do you really know them that well? What do you think they would say about you if they were asked questions? Do you think they would know enough about you to be able to answer the question fully? The chances are that they won't. They're missing out, however, because underneath it all, you're a warm and funny person, someone whose enthusiasm is very infectious.

In baby steps, thinking about those people around you on a daily basis, try your best to open up a little, step by step. You can do this by offering up small details of what you did at the weekend, maybe talking about your family on occasion, basically chatting about the small things in life, which comes together to help us get to know the people around us. Your private nature isn't being breached here because you're not talking about your deepest, darkest secrets, just the small details that make you the person that you are.

Don't try and do too much at one time here, because by pushing yourself out there, it could come over as false. You need to be comfortable, in order for people to understand that you're being genuine and not conceited. Remember that people aren't used to you being this open, and the change may be confusing at first!

5
Learn to Plan a Little

One of the most frustrating things about dealing with an ISTP personality type in your life, especially if in a relationship with one, is their inability to plan anything!

You might recognize this trait in yourself, but you are so laid back that you are practically horizontal, and you don't like to plan anything, preferring just to let life happen. That's all very well and good in many ways, but sometimes you need to plan things, in order to make positive changes in your life! It's a vicious circle in many ways.

Let's check out the positive side of this trait first.

Being so relaxed, you do not stress or worry about much in life; you go with the flow, you let life happen, and you understand that you can't control or change everything that is sent your way. This means that your life is likely to be quite chilled out as a result, and you're not going to start overthinking anything and getting yourself wound up for no reason. We know that stress is not a healthy thing to have in your life, and as an ISTP, you don't tend to suffer from this very often, if at all.

Many people are attracted to this laid-back demeanor of yours because they are envious of your inability to worry. Someone who overthinks a lot, worries about everything, and deals with anxiety is likely to wish they could be more like you, because it allows you to take joy in the smaller things in life, without stressing about things that don't need to be stressed about. There is nothing about that side of it all.

Now, what is the downside? We've listed this as a positive and a negative. Firstly, the positive is what we have just mentioned, the lack of stress and worry in your life. The negative side is that if you don't make plans, if you don't put these plans into action, life can become a little, well, static.

Whilst there are opportunities in life which just happen out of the blue, these are also very few and far between. We have to put in the work if we want the thing to happen in our life. For instance, if you have always dreamed of becoming a doctor, it's no good sitting around waiting for a medical contract to fall into your lap. You need to train, you need to apply for jobs, and you need to work had to get to where you need to be. Life is not just going to rain down a medical job opening for you. Whilst there is a certain amount of magic in life, it's really not the Harry Potter set!

Another more lifestyle-based example is if you want to lose weight because you're not really that happy with your current size. Now, it's admirable to be laid back about it, in an 'I'll try but I'm not going to make myself unhappy doing it' kind of way, but if you don't make a positive plan and put it into action, nothing much is going to change. Talking the talk and walking the walks are two very different things, and as an ISTP, you tend to lack in the walking the walk side of it.

If you are in a relationship, the chances are that your partner will list your inability to make plans as one of the things that they find frustrating or even upsetting to you. You see, it's all very well and good being relaxed, but sometimes there is a real need to plan, and to do something about said plan too. If this part of your personality is the area you need to work on most, you could be putting yourself at risk of losing important people in your life, because they become frustrated with your lack of looking forward. They don't realize that you do want those things too, it's just that you don't see the sense in rushing.

The Fear of Commitment

Another trait which features in the ISTP category is a fear of commitment. We will talk about this issue in this particular chapter because it ties in quite well with the planning subject too. Again, remember this is nothing finger pointing here, we are simply highlighting the issues that may be a problem for you.

You, as we have mentioned, like to go day-by-day and let life happen, and that means that planning and committing to anything goes against the mindset. Again, if you are in a relationship with someone, they could become a little frustrated by your seeming lack of interest in making any future plans. It's important to help them to see that it's not that you don't want to commit to them, and that you have committed to them already in your own way, it's just that you don't like to be tied down in a traditional way. This isn't a reflection on them or your relationship, it's just the laid-back way that makes it comfortable for you to live your life. If that person is okay with this, then

you've found a keeper, but if they're not, you need to
reach a compromise or risk losing them altogether.

At some point in life, you have to say 'this is what I
want', and 'this is what I am going to do about getting
it'. So, what do you want to achieve in your life? What
are your dreams? How badly do you want them to
happen?

Think about this and write it down. Next, what can
you do to achieve them? Don't worry, you're not
writing a strict itinerary of life here, you're just giving
yourself ideas and a plan of action that you can put
into place at your own speed and pace, to get you
where you want to go. Do you need to go out and
find a special someone? Do you need to open up a
little more and let someone in? Do you need to
propose to your partner? What is it that is going to
get you where you need to be?

The next thing is to think about what you don't want.
It's likely that your 'going with the flow' has to lead to
a few unwanted things in your life. Planning and
making commitments is just as much about the things
you don't want, as the things you do. If you can
identify these and put into place a plan to kick them
out of your life, you'll be much happier as a result.
Think of this as a liver detox, rather than a planning
exercise.

Life is not something which just happens to you, it is
something which you have a certain amount of
control over if you choose to plan and work towards
it. This is the main point you should take away from
this chapter if nothing else.

6
Learn to Concentrate on One Thing until Completion

A brilliant mind is rarely set on one thing at any one time, and instead, it begins to flits from one thing to another, filling the brain with all manner of interesting facts and experiences. It's total sensory overload, but in a good way too.

As an ISTP, this sums you up perfectly!

Up to now, we have talked about how you are a spontaneous person, and that is something we are going to explore in much more detail in our next chapter. What we're going to talk about now, however, is the fact that as an ISTP, you are likely to jump from one thing to another, without really finishing the task. This can be frustrating for you sometimes, but especially for those around you!

We first need to think about why this happens in the first place.

You are a creative person, and you want to know how things work. This means that your mind is full of wonder and excitement when you see something new. You become so engrossed in it that you pour all your attention into that one project. Once you find out what you need to know, you're likely to want to share what you've learned with those around you. That's great, after all. Then? Then you leave the project and have your head turned into something else.

As you can see, the end result, the actual final result, never actually gets performed, i.e. putting the thing back together again.

You can learn so much more by finishing a job to total completion, and this will really help to fulfill your wonder and curiosity in life. Try and ignore the urge to walk away from a project once it loses its shine, and instead push through to the end, sure, in the knowledge that there is more to be learned. There usually is, after all.

ISTP's are quite easily bored – that is the best way, to sum up, the situation.

So, how can you curb this easy boredom tendency?

We certainly don't want to curb your appetite for learning new things and your wonder for how things work because this is one of the main strengths and positive items in your personality type. When learning how to enhance your personality type, it's always important to remember not to curb a strength, when trying to fix a weakness. The best way to address this particular weakness, therefore, is to work in baby steps.

If you are aware of this potential issue, then you can do something about it when you notice it coming into effect. For instance, when you are working on something, i.e. when you trying to learn how something works, keep at the back of your mind that you do have this tendency to become bored with a project as it is nearing completion. You don't have to do anything about it at this stage, you simply need to be mindful of it, that's all.

When you notice the urge to walk away from the project becoming stronger, drag that mindfulness towards the front of your brain and become even more aware of it. Tell yourself that there is more to be learned by continuing on to the very end. You're not lying to yourself after all, because who knows what else there is to be discovered?

You will also find a sense of achievement by actually finishing a task, and you won't feel as overwhelmed. Having said that, as an ISTP, it's unlikely that you feel stressed out by issues such as this, but over time, having several unfinished things on your to-do list can become overwhelming, to say the least.

Practice is going to make perfect here, and that is the case with many activities we're talking about as we explore the ISTP personality type. You're quite a complex being, in that you're so reserved and private, but you're so enthusiastic and open to learning at the same time. Your creative nature makes that paradox so fascinating, but when you're trying to learn how to develop your strengths and minimise your weaknesses, it's important to realize that it's not going to happen overnight – practice and perseverance is the way forward.

7
Learn to Curb Your Unpredictability

Life is certainly not dull or boring when you're side by side with an ISTP! You are someone who loves to explore, and that spontaneous urge in your personality means that you're likely to just up sticks and head off somewhere new, on a mission to seek out knowledge and truth.

How exciting!

The downside? Life is not designed to be lived completely spontaneously because life is about predictability in some ways.

In a previous chapter, we talked about how you don't like to be tied down, and you don't like to plan, and we gave you some practical ways to try and change that part of your personality to some degree. This chapter is designed to build on that, working hand in hand with the subject matter.

There is nothing dull about routine, provided that routine gives you enough scope for adventure and exploration too. We have to pay bills, we have to go to work, we have to do the cleaning; routine is what stops life from being chaotic and out of order, it is what stops stress and unpredictability from becoming a massive problem. If you live your life completely spontaneously, then you're running the risk of everything spiraling out of control.

Now, as an ISTP, you are not reckless or irresponsible, it's just that sometimes your spontaneous nature leads you into situations that you would rather not be in. Having said that, sometimes you do have a talent for resisting those spontaneous urges – another total contradiction of the ISTP personality type!

The way through all of this? Being mindful of the situations you are in.

The fact that you are reading this book means that you are now aware of the fact that you do have a tendency towards the spontaneous. Knowing about this is the first step. Now, it's also very important to realize that we don't want to take away this spontaneous element completely because a little spontaneity in life is sometimes a good thing! It's simply important to know when to be spontaneous and when to curb it a little.

Stop and think. Ask yourself these questions.

- Is this really a good idea?
- What will I gain by doing this?
- What are the potential downsides?
- Is there any danger involved?

If you give yourself the chance to think about the action your spontaneous nature is trying to make you do, it may lose its shine. If it doesn't, and there is no danger to be had, then go ahead, by all means!

If life was lived completely spontaneously, e.g. if we
never had any planning through about anything, then
it would be, as we mentioned before, chaotic. We
would miss payments on important bills, and then we
would find that our electricity or Internet connection
would be cut off. We would miss important meetings,
and we may lose our jobs as a result. We would upset
people close to us because we would miss out on
those things we promised we would do.

As you can see, sometimes routine is important, and
sometimes unpredictability is the best course of
action.

You are not a planner, this is something we know,
and whilst flying by the seat of your pants in some
situations is a good route towards success, it is rarely
the best course of action for everything in life.
Learning to appreciate predictability is something that
can be done, and if you can combine it with the
occasional spontaneous episode, which is safe and
questioned before it is done, then you really will have
found the key to a full and fulfilling life.

8
Conclusion

And there we have it, the creative and sometimes unpredictable world of the ISTP!

Remember that there is no intention in any of this book to paint a negative picture of your personality type. You are a very creative and wonderful soul, you are someone who is packed with excitement and wonder for how things work in life, and because of all that, you are someone we can all learn from in many ways. Every single one of us has weaknesses, it is what makes us human, but the important thing is to know about them and learn to stop them from holding us back in life.

Your strengths should certainly be celebrated. There aren't many people out there who can be so laid back and chilled out on one hand, and so spontaneously charged on the other! You are a contradiction, you are the virtuoso! You are a fun person to know, and you are an interesting person to understand. Of course, you don't let people in very easily, but if you can learn to open up just a little, and allow those people to get to know the real you, then you'll find that life becomes ten times more fun, and ten times more interesting as a result.

Remember to read about the other personality types in the spectrum too, because you are very unlikely to be 100% ISTP. If you are, that's great, but most of us do air on the side of other types from time to time too. It's also really useful to learn about these different types from a social point of view because it allows us to understand other people in much more detail overall. You'll find your relationships, both personal and professional will be more fulfilling and rewarding as a result.

The overall aim of this book is to allow you to totally appreciate your ISTP nature to the maximum, to celebrate your strengths and understand your weaknesses. If you can do that, and if you can work to minimize those weaknesses and the impact they may have on different areas of your life, you're well on your way to becoming a well-rounded, positive, and happy human being!

Note from the author

Thank you for purchasing and reading this book. If you enjoyed it or found it useful then I'd really appreciate it if you would post a short review on Amazon. I do read all the reviews personally so that I can continually write what people are wanting.

If you'd like to leave a review then please visit the link below:

https://www.amazon.com/dp/B078Z7GGBP

Thanks for your support and good luck!

Check Out My Other Books

Below you'll find some of my other books that are popular on Amazon and Kindle as well. Simply search the titles listed below on Amazon. Alternatively, you can visit my author page on Amazon to see other work done by me.

ENFP: Understand and Break Free From Your Own Limitations

INFP: Understand and Break Free From Your Own Limitations

ENFJ: Understand and Break Free From Your Own Limitations

INFJ: Understand and Break Free From Your Own Limitations

ENFP: INFP: ENFJ: INFJ: Understand and Break Free From Your Own Limitations – The Diplomat Bundle Series

INTP: Understand and Break Free From Your Own Limitations

INTJ: Understand and Break Free From Your Own Limitations

ENTP: Understand and Break Free From Your Own Limitations

ENTJ: Understand and Break Free From Your Own Limitations

ESTJ: Understand and Break Free From Your Own Limitations

ISTJ: Understand and Break Free From Your Own Limitations

ISFJ: Understand and Break Free From Your Own Limitations

ESFJ: Understand and Break Free From Your Own Limitations

OPTION B: F**K IT - How to Finally Take Control Of Your Life And Break Free From All Expectations. Live A Limitless, Fearless, Purpose Driven Life With Ultimate Freedom

www.ingramcontent.com/pod-product-compliance
Lightning Source LLC
Chambersburg PA
CBHW021148260726
48656CB00025B/2246